Are you on the right road to knowing God?

Rob and Lisa Laizure

ONE WAY
Are you on the right road to knowing God?

By Rob & Lisa Laizure

Copyright © 2013 by Rob and Lisa Laizure
Revised 2014

Previous Title – Got Heaven?
by Rob and Lisa Laizure

Printed in the United States

ISBN 978-0-9839929-2-9

All rights reserved solely by the author. The author guarantees all contents are original and do not infringe upon the legal rights of any other person or work. No part of this book may be reproduced in any form without the permission of the author. The views expressed in this book are not necessarily those of the publisher.

Unless otherwise indicated, all scripture verses are from:
Copyright © 1992–2011 Logos Bible Software.

The Holy Bible, Libronix NASB Version

ConnectingTheDotsMinistries.com

Rob and Lisa Laizure have authored several other books:

Connecting the Dots

Discouraged

Growing Faith

Teamwork

The Holy Land

The Truth About Marriage

True or False

The Equation

ConnectingTheDotsMinistries.com

Table of Contents

1. The world today 9
2. How many ways are there to heaven? 13
3. Saved from what? 17
4. The plan of God 21
5. What is my part? 25
6. Pictures from the war 29
7. Heaven or hell 31
8. Decision time 37
9. What next? 39

CHAPTER 1

The world today

Heaven or hell — fact or fiction? Seemingly, these are age-old topics of conversation in a world of endless turmoil — wars over religious beliefs, the World Trade Centers crumbling to the ground, and religious fanatics believing they will be ushered into heaven when they die a martyr's death. Is this true? Do people go to heaven if they are sincere about their belief system? Are all religious people going to be there? What is true? Is there an absolute truth in this world we can stand on and have hope in?

Our answer would be, "Yes, there is a truth, and yes, we can have hope." Finding that truth in the world today is a difficult task. Turn on the TV or radio talk shows and you will be told the road to heaven is very wide and all-inclusive. "Just be a good person," "Just believe in God," "Just go to church," and everything will be okay. Some say it doesn't matter what you believe in as long as you are sincere. But is it possible to be a sincerely religious person and be sincerely wrong? What does it truly mean to know God and to know with absolute certainty that you will spend eternity in heaven?

We have a friend who owns a mortuary. She told us that for all the 20 years she has been doing funerals, mourners believe that every one of the dearly departed has gone to heaven. We had a friend who died at a young age, and the service centered on the fact that even though he was dead, he must be up in heaven playing golf. After each of these memorials, friends and family walked out feeling that the person who just died was heaven-bound, and yet, is that possible in every instance? How likely is it that a person that passed away, who never believed in God and was not concerned for the things of God, would be in heaven today?

For the answers to these questions we will turn to the Bible. **2 Timothy 3:16 says, "All Scripture is given by inspiration of God, and is profitable for doctrine, for reproof, for correction, for instruction in righteousness, that the man of God may be complete, thoroughly equipped for every good work."**

The Bible was inspired by God, or in other words, "God-breathed." He moved in the hearts of 40 writers over 2000 years of time to record the history of mankind, how sin has infected this world, and how man is separated from God because of this sin. The Old Testament points toward a day when there would come a Savior who would take away these sins. The New Testament introduces this Savior as Jesus Christ, the perfect, sinless man who is God, and who would die on a cross to pay the penalty for our sins. Jesus arose from the dead three days after His death; an act which would show the world that He is God and has conquered death for those who put their faith and trust in Him.

The Bible gives us all the information we need to know about life, how to live, and where we will go after we die.

Psalm 119:105 says, **"Your word is a lamp to my feet and a light to my path."**

As we walk through life, it seems as if there is darkness all around. The Bible, however, gives us the light we need to walk; therefore, it is worth spending time to see what it has to say to us.

CHAPTER 2

How many ways are there to heaven?

One day I spoke with someone that I assumed was a Christian because she went to church regularly and helped the homeless. She had a family member who was marrying into a non-Christian religion and I told her my concerns about it. She proceeded to tell me she would rather her relative marry into any religion than not to believe in God at all. As the conversation went on, I proceeded to tell her that the Bible clearly stated there was only ONE WAY to God and that is through a relationship with Jesus Christ.

In **John 14:6**, the Bible clearly says, **"Jesus said to him, 'I am the way, the truth, and the life. No one comes to the Father except through Me.'"**

Again, in **Acts 4:12, "Nor is there salvation in any other, for there is no other name under heaven given among men by which we must be saved."**

Her response was to tell me how narrow-minded that was, and if I truly believed these verses, then I would be disregarding three-fourths of the religions of the world. As I got off the phone, I had to keep reminding myself that these are God's rules, not mine. This is His plan for salvation, not mine. If He says Jesus is the only way to heaven, then I cannot argue with what He says in His Word, the Bible.

Unfortunately, people do not want to take the Bible as their final authority. We hear dozens of excuses why people refuse to believe the Bible. Here are just a few:

- "It has been translated so many times that it can't be right."

- "It was meant for a time long ago; it is not relevant for today."

- "Nobody can truly understand what the Bible really means."

The problem actually begins with a lack of knowledge about God. If we have a small view of God then it makes sense that we wouldn't believe He is able to protect His Word that He has given us. If He is some distant deity that is powerless, then it seems plausible that the Bible has not been preserved because God is not able.

But, if we have a high view of God, a true biblical view of God, we would know for certain that He is more than capable of protecting what He has given us. If He created this world and everything in it, wouldn't He be able to make certain the Bible – His Word to us – would be translated correctly? If He is all-knowing, all-seeing, and all-powerful, couldn't He make sure of this?

You would be surprised at how relevant the Bible is to all of us living today. It addresses who God is and how He affects our lives. It deals with every issue of the past, the present, and the future. Everything we need to know about God and His plan for this world and our lives is written in the pages of the Bible.

Understanding the Bible is not really as hard as people think it is. The problem in our day and age is that most people simply do not take the time to read it. Most of it is basic, but some passages will take extra time to study. Studying the Bible is just like what happens when a child is growing. They learn things slowly at first and with each year of their life, they are capable of learning more. It is the same with reading and learning from the Bible: it takes time and is a process.

The first step in answering the question, "How many ways are there to heaven?" would be to understand the Bible and to accept the Bible as your final authority. The absolute fact of the Bible is this – Jesus is the only way to God. From the beginning of time, the plan of God was to save His people. We once had a man ask what he needed to be "saved from." This is a critical question, so we will deal with this next.

CHAPTER 3

Saved from what?

The answer to the question "saved from what?" would be the word "sin." In the culture we live in today, this does not seem to be a subject we like to talk about. But the Bible does talk about it, and in a very specific way.

From the moment Adam and Eve ate the fruit in the garden and disobeyed God, sin came into being. **Romans 5:12** says, **"Therefore, just as through one man sin entered the world, and death through sin, and thus death spread to all men, because all sinned."** The absolute truth is we are born sinners – not some of us, but all of us. **Romans 3:23** states, **"for ALL have sinned and fall short of the glory of God"** (Emphasis added).

The Bible goes on to explain what happens because of this sin. **Romans 6:23** tells us, **"For the wages of sin is death, but the gift of God is eternal life in Christ Jesus our Lord."** The Bible says we are born sinners, and because of that fact, we will die separated from God. So what exactly is sin? Sin means "missing the mark" or in other words, being disobedient to the laws of God. Many of us were raised in a home where sin was rarely talked about. We were likely not told the true reason for our need to know Christ which was this: we have a problem. This problem was something that separated us from God. This problem was something we were born with.

Becoming a Christian begins with understanding that Jesus died on the cross for a specific reason. Since sin leads to death for all, God had a plan from the beginning of time. In the Old Testament, sins were paid for by animal sacrifices. There had to be blood shed as payment for disobedience to God. **Hebrews 9:22 says, "And according to the law almost all things are purified with blood, and without the shedding of blood there is no remission."**

God's design for salvation was this: Jesus, who was God, would be born to a virgin, live a completely sinless life and take our sins upon Himself. Once we accepted what He did for us, we would be holy and blameless in God's sight. In **2 Corinthians 5:21**, the Bible says, **"For He made Him who knew no sin to be sin for us, that we might become the righteousness of God in Him."** God says that Jesus, who had no sin in His life, took our sins on Himself so we could be righteous in His sight. That is God working out His perfect plan to save us.

In order to be a Christian, the first step is to understand this fact. "I am a sinner in desperate need of a way out of the punishment my sins deserve. That punishment would be death – that is, death in the form of separation from God when I die. The way out was provided by the sacrificial death and resurrection of Jesus."

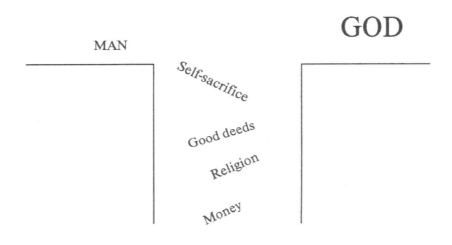

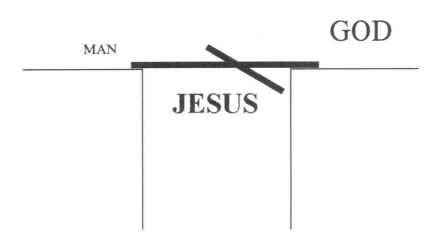

Diagram: The chasm separating man from God and His holiness.

Think of it as our being on one side of the Grand Canyon and God is on the other. No matter how hard we try to jump to the other side, it is impossible. We can be good and moral people, we can go to church, we can help the needy, but there is still an impossible chasm between God and us. We cannot bridge this gap on our own (see diagram).

Isaiah 64:6a says, **(NLT)**

> **"We are all infected and impure with sin. When we display our righteous deeds, they are nothing but filthy rags."**

God's view of us is so different from our view of ourselves. He looks at all our righteous acts as "filthy rags." He looks at all the good things we do as futile, useless attempts to bridge the gap to God. But on our own we can't. We are hopeless and we are helpless. Rarely are we told the truth about our condition—which is that we are all sinners.

This is the first step to understanding what it truly means to be a follower of Christ. We need to humbly realize we are not good enough to ever stand in the presence of a holy God. Mercifully, God has a plan.

CHAPTER 4

The plan of God

Thankfully, God had a way to bridge the chasm, the impossible gap between Him and all of us. It was done through His Son, Jesus Christ. **John 3:16** tells us of His great love for us: **"For God so loved the world that He gave His only begotten Son, that whoever believes in Him should not perish but have everlasting life." Romans 5:8** says, **"But God demonstrates His own love towards us, in that while we were still sinners, Christ died for us."** 2 Corinthians 5:21 exhorts, **"For He made Him who knew no sin to be sin for us, that we might become the righteousness of God in Him."**

Jesus came to earth, lived a perfect, sinless life, took our sins on Himself and exchanged His righteousness for our sinfulness. No more condemnation. No more guilt. No more shame. Thankfully the chasm has been bridged by Jesus—not by a church, not by a tradition and not by anything you or I could do. **Ephesians 2:8-9** states, **"For by grace you have been saved, through faith, and that not of yourselves; it is a gift of God, not of works, lest anyone should**

boast." In other words, I cannot do anything. God does everything instead. We like to think of this as the "great exchange" – my sinfulness for His righteousness.

What separates Christianity from many other religions is that Jesus Christ arose from the dead and is alive. If you research other religions, you will find the leaders of those religions are dead. Christianity means life; life after death because Jesus conquered death.

We are such a "works" oriented society. We are taught that the harder we work, the more money we make and the farther we can go up the corporate ladder. The problem with this mindset is that in God's economy the opposite is true. Salvation is a gift, not something we can work for. That is hard for us to understand and accept. We can't imagine how something as important as where we go when we die is a gift and can't be earned. But this is what the Bible says, and if we take the Bible as our final authority, we have to believe what it says. **Acts 2:23-24** says, **"Him [Jesus], being delivered by the determined purpose and foreknowledge of God, you have taken by lawless hands, have crucified, and put to death; whom God raised up, having loosed the pains of death, because it was not possible that He should be held by it."**

That is why Easter is such a celebration for Christians. Without the resurrection, our faith would be in vain; it would be useless. If Jesus had not risen from the dead, we would be trusting our salvation to a man no different from us. But the Bible says this man, Jesus Christ, was God.

John 1:1 says, **"In the beginning was the Word, and the Word was with God, and the Word was God."**

John 1:14 explains further, **"And the Word became flesh and dwelt among us, and we beheld His glory, the glory as of the only begotten of the Father, full of grace and truth."**

Because Jesus is God, He has the ability to take our sins upon Himself and exchange our sin for His perfect, sinless life. When He arose from the dead, He conquered death and enabled us to conquer death also. Putting our faith and trust in what He did for us is the key factor in becoming a Christian.

CHAPTER 5

What is my part?

Our part in this plan is simple: believe and repent. What does it mean to truly believe? Does a person just have to believe God exists? Can I mentally assent to this fact by itself and be a Christian?

The answer is found in **James 2:19** which says, **"You believe that there is one God. You do well. Even the demons believe – and tremble!"**

Belief in Jesus must move from your head to your heart. What would differentiate between your belief in Jesus and a demon's belief in Jesus? When you understand the truth of what Jesus did on the cross for you and you accept the fact that this is a gift from God, you become full of gratitude- gratitude for what He has done to give you a new life, gratitude for the ability to be forgiven, gratitude for knowing you will spend eternity in heaven. Suddenly, you are bursting with a new life full of freedom and peace. This belief does not stay in your head but rather it moves you on to a new life.

The Bible says in **Matthew 4:17, "From that time Jesus began to preach and to say, 'Repent, for the kingdom of heaven is at hand.'"**

Belief is the beginning and repentance is the next step. As you start to live out your new life, you will begin to understand what the Bible means in **2 Corinthians 5:17** when it explains, **"Therefore, if anyone is in Christ, he is a new creation; old things have passed away; behold, all things have become new."**

Repentance is simply turning away from sin. When you acknowledge that Jesus as the only way to God and accept His free gift of salvation, then your new life begins. **Ezekiel 36:26** says, **"I will give you a new heart and put a new spirit within you; I will take the heart of stone out of your flesh and give you a heart of flesh. I will put My Spirit within you and cause you to walk in My statues and you will keep My judgments and do them."** When you put your trust in Jesus for both your earthly life and your eternal life, He promises to give you a new heart. He promises to put His Spirit in you and cause you to walk in His ways! With a new life comes a new heart. With a new heart comes a new way of life. Your old life is gone and God will make and mold you to look like His Son, Jesus.

We read of a woman who all her life thought she was a Christian. She taught Sunday School and she went to church so she thought she was spiritually fine, but at the age of 29 she realized her life was a mess. She lived to please herself and she lived her life accordingly. She didn't love God or His Word and she was deeply involved in sin, yet the moment she came humbly before God and truly gave her life to Him, things changed. She discovered she now had the desire and the ability to say "no" to sin. She gained an abounding love for God and His Word. She found herself grateful for being saved. She gained insight into the Bible as she read it. Her life now had the evidence of giving her heart and mind to Jesus. The same thing can happen for you. Believe and repent. Turn from the things that offend God, and because He gives you a new heart, the things that offended Him will now offend you. That is what it means to be a true Christian.

We know people who believe that because they "prayed a quick prayer" or "walked down an aisle" when they were younger that they are truly Christians. They believe they can acknowledge a relationship with Jesus in spite of the fact that nothing in their life has ever changed. They live for themselves. They have no time for the things of God. They have no desire to read the Bible. Nowhere does the Bible say this behavior is the behavior of a Christian.

1 John 2:19 says: **"They went out from us, but they were not really of us; for if they had been of us, they would have remained with us; but they went out, so that it would be shown that they all are not of us."**

Philippians 1:6 says, **"being confident of this very thing, that He who began a good work in you will complete it until the day of Jesus Christ."**

We had a man ask us, "But doesn't the Bible just say, 'Believe on the Lord Jesus and you will be saved?'" We said it does, but unfortunately, we cannot take one verse out of the whole Bible and stand or fall on it. It does say that very thing, but it also says we have to repent.

It says in **John 14:15, "If you love Me, keep My commandments."**

John 8:31-32 says, **"…if you abide in My word, you are My disciples indeed. And you shall know the truth, and the truth shall make you free."**

1 Corinthians 6:9-11 tells us that there must be a life change:

"Do you not know that the unrighteous will not inherit the kingdom of God? Do not be deceived. Neither fornicators, nor idolaters, nor adulterers, nor homosexuals, nor sodomites, nor thieves, nor covetous, nor drunkards, nor revilers, nor extortioners will inherit the kingdom of God. And such WERE some of you. But you were washed, but you were sanctified, but you were justified in the name of the Lord Jesus and by the Spirit of our God" (Emphasis added).

Being a Christian means a new life. We are able to forget our past and start afresh. Through Him, we become new creatures in Christ. We owe our lives to Jesus for what He did for us. We get a new heart, we learn to love Him, and we will spend eternity in heaven.

CHAPTER 6

Pictures from the war

As we are writing this, the war in Iraq has just started. We got a visual image of true salvation as we watched the first pictures come in on our television. We saw a picture of a Marine standing over two men who were on their knees waving a white flag in surrender. The Marine was there for one purpose-to save them. He wanted to give them a new life, a new hope for the future. The two men surrendering were so humble, realizing that this Marine was their only hope. They had been in bondage to an evil regime for so long that to surrender could have cost them their lives, but they were willing to pay any price. They were tired of living under evil and ready to give up whatever they had to in order to have better lives.

True surrender will only be realized after the war is over. Will these men go back to their old way of life without a thought for the Marine who made their freedom possible? Will they mock him to their friends? Will it have been a surrender based on a feeling for the moment? A true surrender means a changed life. Everything in the lives of the two men from that minute forward will change. Will they be grateful for their freedom? Will they forever live their lives in light of their new freedom? They cannot ever go back to their former lives. They have been set free. They owe their lives to the Marine who risked his life to give them a new life. Can they ever be the same? In light of the gracious gift of a new life from the Marine, they will forever be changed.

That is a picture of what Jesus does for us. He sees us helpless, hopeless, and lost in our sin. He sees us bound to our evil, sinful nature, and He wants to set us free. We have been living under the evil regime of Satan. Jesus wants to give us a new life with all the freedom of knowing and loving Him. He wants us to live with Him forever in heaven. He wants to give us joy and peace in all circumstances.

He promises in **Romans 8:28** that **"...all things work together for good to those who love God, who are the called according to His purpose."**

He promises us an abundant life – not a perfect life or a pain free life, but a life with a purpose, knowing He is in control. Will you surrender? Will you see your life as hopeless without Jesus' coming and setting you free? Better yet, will your surrender be true? Will you live your life in total surrender to Jesus for dying on the cross for you? He is there to give you life. He isn't there to harm you. He is there to give you the greatest gift of all – salvation which brings eternal life, hope, and peace. All you need do is raise your white flag and surrender and let God do the rest.

CHAPTER 7

Heaven or hell

People tend to minimize the idea of hell. Some tend to make it out to be a better place than it is, assuming they will be able to spend eternity with their friends in a party-like atmosphere. For most of us, it is hard to believe such a place exists. But remember, if we take the Bible as our final authority, we do not have the option to question if hell is a reality. The Bible says it is real and is not a place you would want to spend eternity. Here are some verses that explain what it will be like:

> **Matthew 25:41**
> "Then He will also say to those on the left hand, 'Depart from Me, you cursed, into the everlasting fire prepared for the devil and his angels.'"

> **Matthew 25:46**
> "These will go away into eternal punishment, but the righteous into eternal life."

Revelation 14:9-11
> "If anyone worships the beast and his image, and receives his mark on his forehead or on his hand, he himself shall also drink of the wine of the wrath of God, which is poured out full strength into the cup of His indignation. He shall be tormented with fire and brimstone in the presence of the holy angels and in the presence of the Lamb. And the smoke of their torment ascends forever and ever; and they have no rest day or night, who worship the beast and his image, and whoever receives the mark of his name."

Here in the Bible you will find the truth about hell- torment, no rest day and night, everlasting fire, eternal punishment. This is not the fun place many people believe it will be. Sadly, many of us do not want to tell others about the consequences of not believing in Jesus, but instead we tend to focus on explaining God's mercy and grace.

The problem with this is that only part of the Bible is revealed. God is loving and kind, but He is also holy, with an absolute hatred of sin. His wrath will be poured out on sin, and if you are one of those who has not given your life to Jesus and allowed Him to take the penalty for your sin, then you will spend eternity separated from God in the place called hell.

This by far is the most serious and important question you will ever have to answer: "Do you know where you are going when you die?"

If, on the other hand, you have given yourself completely to Jesus and surrendered your entire life to Him, you can be assured of the answer to the question, "Where will I go when I die?" The answer is heaven. Here are some verses that talk about what heaven is like:

Revelation 21:4
> "And God will wipe away every tear from their eyes; there shall be no more death, nor sorrow, nor crying. There shall be no more pain, for the former things have passed away."

John 14:1-2
> "Let not your heart be troubled; you believe in God, believe also in Me. In My Father's house are many mansions; if it were not so, I would have told you. I go to prepare a place for you."

Luke 23:42-43
> "Then he said to Jesus, 'Lord, remember me when You come into Your kingdom.' And Jesus said to him, 'Assuredly, I say to you, today you will be with Me in Paradise.'"

Revelation 7:16-17
> "They shall neither hunger anymore nor thirst anymore; the sun shall not strike them, nor any heat; for the Lamb who is in the midst of the throne will shepherd them and lead them to living fountains

of waters. And God will wipe away every tear from their eyes."

Revelation 22:1
"And he showed me a pure river of water of life, clear as crystal, proceeding from the throne of God and of the Lamb."

Revelation 22:5
"There shall be no night there; they need no lamp nor light of the sun, for the Lord God gives them light. And they shall reign forever and ever."

As you can see from these verses, the difference between heaven and hell is astonishing. Heaven is peaceful, with no sorrow or pain. Heaven is referred to as Paradise. It is filled with mansions, and light without any darkness at all. This is such a contrast to what the Bible says about hell.

If you have given your life to Jesus, **1 John 5:12-13** promises:

> "He who has the Son has life; he who does not have the Son of God does not have life. These things I have written to you who believe in the name of the Son of God, that you MAY KNOW THAT YOU HAVE ETERNAL LIFE, and that you may continue to believe in the name of the Son of God." (Emphasis added).

Stand on this promise.

John 10:28 says, **"And I give them eternal life, and they shall never perish; neither shall anyone snatch them out of My hand."**

He promises to draw you to Himself, change your life, and give you eternal life. What more could we ever ask?

CHAPTER 8

Decision time

As you can see from the following verse, the way to heaven is a narrow road. **Matthew 7:13** tells us to **"Enter by the narrow gate; for wide is the gate and broad is the way that leads to destruction, and there are many who go in by it. Because narrow is the gate and difficult is the way which leads to life, and there are few who find it."**

The Bible says the road to God is narrow and very few will find it. It shows the way to hell being broad, wide, and all-inclusive. If we are going to take the Bible as God's Word to us and the final authority in our lives, then we must believe what it says. There is only one way that leads to a changed life and then eternal life: Jesus. What decision will you make?

The Bible says in **1 Corinthians 1:18, "For the message of the cross is foolishness to those who are perishing, but to us who are being saved it is the power of God."**

Is the thought of Jesus being the only way to God foolishness to you? If so, the Bible says you are perishing.

John 6:44 explains, **"No one can come to Me unless the Father who sent Me draws him; and I will raise him up at the last day."**

Is this making sense to you for the first time in your life? Do you feel a tugging at your heart? That would be God drawing you. Tell Him that you know you are a sinner in need of a Savior. Tell Him that you know Jesus is the only way to Him. Humbly ask Him to forgive your sins and change your life, and you will be amazed at what He will do.

John 1:12
"But as many as received Him, to them He gave the right to become children of God, even to those who believe in His name."

CHAPTER 9

What next?

To help you start your new life, pick up a Bible and start reading. God promises in **Isaiah 55:11, "So shall My word be that goes forth from My mouth; it shall not return to Me void, but it shall accomplish what I please, and it shall prosper in the thing for which I sent it."**

In **Hebrews 4:12** the Bible states, **"For the word of God is living and powerful, and sharper than any two edged sword, piercing even to the division of soul and spirit, and of joints and marrow, and is a discerner of the thoughts and intents of the heart."**

The Bible is what God uses to change our lives. Here are a few steps to help you grow in your faith.

- Buy a Bible that is an easy translation to read such as the New Living Translation. Start with the Gospel of John in the New Testament. As you read it, do so with a heart open to change.

- Find a Bible-teaching church. This is extremely important. We hear many people say they do not need to go to church, that they worship on their own. The Bible says in **Hebrews 10:24-25 "And let us consider one another in order to stir up love and good works, not forsaking the assembling of ourselves together, as is the manner of some, but exhorting one another and so much the more as you see the Day approaching."**

When 3,000 people became Christians in one day in Acts 2:41, the next thing they did was stated in **Acts 2:42 "And they continued steadfastly in the apostles' doctrine and fellowship, in the breaking of bread and in prayers."** They had church. This is the natural progression after becoming a Christian. Find a church that teaches what the Bible says. God uses pastors and teachers to help you understand His word.

- Find a small men's Bible study or women's Bible study. Make friends who truly love God. Find someone who can answer your questions.

- Pray. Prayer is just talking to God. Tell Him how you feel. Pray for your friends and relatives. Pray that He will open your eyes to the truths in the Bible. Pray that your life would change and be pleasing to Him.

- Be baptized. The Bible makes it clear as a Christian we need to be baptized to make a public confession of our faith.

Acts 2:41
   "So then, those who had received his word

were baptized; and that day there were
added about three thousand souls."

Acts 19:4-5, Paul said, **"John baptized with the baptism of repentance, telling the people to believe in Him who was coming after him, that is, in Jesus."** When they heard this, they were baptized in the name of the Lord Jesus.

- Join a small group or community group with your church so you can meet other Christians and grow in your faith.

Matthew 22:37 says, **"Jesus said to him, 'You shall love the Lord your God with all your heart, with all your soul, and with all your mind.'"**

Our hope and prayer is that as you surrender your life to Jesus, this verse will become the focal point of your new life in Christ. The only way to love Him with all your heart, soul, and mind is to spend the time getting to know Him. Your growth as a new Christian will be determined by how much time you spend reading the Bible and learning who He is and how He can affect your life.

The Bible says there is ONE WAY to God…
and that is through Jesus.

All who place their faith and trust in Jesus alone will know Him on earth and spend eternity with Him forever. The Bible, our source of truth, assures us of that with certainty. If you want to know God, just tell Him that you want Jesus in your life. That is the One Way road to knowing God.

If you have any questions or comments, please e-mail us at:

Lisa@WomensBibleStudy.com
or
RobsLaizure@gmail.com

Visit us at our website:
ConnectingTheDotsMinistries.com